SWALLOW THE LAKE

THE WESLEYAN POETRY PROGRAM: VOLUME 54

Swallow the Lake

By

CLARENCE MAJOR

Wesleyan University Press
Middletown, Connecticut

Some of the poems in this book originally appeared in one form or another
in the following publications:

*Anagogic & Paiedeumic Review, Artesian, el corno emplumado, The
Cresset, Down Here, Essence, Fallout, A Houyhnhnm's Scrapbook, Journal
of Black Poetry, Nickel Review, Penny Poems,* and *Works.*

Hardbound: ISBN: 0–8195–2054–3
Paperback: ISBN: 0–8195–1054–8
Library of Congress Catalog Card Number: 79–120258
Manufactured in the United States of America
First Edition

CONTENTS

PART ONE

BLIND OLD WOMAN

spots on black skin.
                she is dry.
how time, how she waits here
in her dingy wool, shabby
                the fingers on her cup.
so frail, a woven face, so oval
such empty charity. how she remains
so quiet, quiet please.
                how the cup shakes. and
it is not straight. nothing
is.
She does not sell candy nor rubber
bands. like the blind man
at the other end. of the silence. the sounds
                of one or two pennies
in the bent up tin. up her canvas stool
at the end of the shadows.
                how they return before her,
through these 1960 Indiana streets.
as she shuffles into street sounds.

MY CHILD

her curls, like black sparkling things
out of the interruptions of music or
endemic structure of just things, are simply
there, not even needing this poem, nor
me: a mirror, coming in my love to what I vainly
interpret as some vague property, a shadow of my-
self, an edge like cement to the city. Her fleecy
soft insides on her face uncommon intrigue so natural
in the brimming domestic shape of her intercourse
with me, enclosed in this ancient respect: her eye-
lids, her 3 year old rendition of the world is
not inferior to anybody's, her play accepts
the debt of herself, the simple undefined reality
of this — .

THE DESIGN

the music and its harmony
measures in the space of my boredom,
remains stale the air, the music.

The house. The things around
the little things around my terms with you.
You never come to terms with
my brain. My music is difficult, you never

empty the ashtrays. I am tired of the
apartment is dull a place but it comes
to this each

item you left, a few belongings: the african woman
with a shrunken leg, one with
a jug, a king dancing. The harmony
does not change the paradox of my birth.

They talk about Mao Tse-tung these days, small
talk, you know. This is simply
a letter of what I might say.

In our cold rooms a mocking laugh
rattles inside the walls. Inside the planks
of our mind, we think alike.

Well, let me tell you
of my new lady. But she says she belongs to
nobody, or the world. A coddle for a poor fool's
pride. And pleasure. Contemporary moments.

Exist, these melodies, difficult phrases, the
            stray bits of speech, exist thru her presence.
SHE HAS COME DOWN
                front, baby. In the spaces, the music.

You say, they say, everybody says, even I say
            the important thing is her virtue: her sins
the building she lives in she lives in
chaos, in roots. In her cracked mirror in her mission
she lives in us, in everybody
            she lives in you.

We live anywhere, by the water, perhaps.
The blade of the water
            does not wake her, cutting her.
When it runs low, the fire sweeps her face but
            does not burn into her sleep. I know
she is peaceful, I

sometimes sleep like a fifteen year old dog
            beside her fire. Warm, losing my touch
I face rough walls in terrible moments, a finger
            might knock the edge, tilt the concerto

but I stop to think. It would be like picking up
a little man, a huge black beard
            weighing down his face, his legs
are goat legs. He sings, like a bird.
And it does not puzzle, nor amaze

any of us. Not even under the effect
of her capsules; she, in her aspects makes no excuses
for such rhythm out of context.

I say it is because of motherhood and she
remains abstract, not giving anything away. Some-
time, like this time
she leaves me feeling as commercial, plastic
as a sunrise on that post card
you sent us from your vacation.

I say to her, Come
into this home, this blue house of black
music. She knows the score
already, she was not as snowed as you, dear.

Now, things are working, we think alike.
No matter what I might say
she is not bored.

SWALLOW THE LAKE

Gave me things I
could not use. Then. Now.
Rain night bursting upon & into. I
shine updown into Lake Michigan

like the glow from the cold lights of the Loop.
Walks. Deaths. Births.
Streets. Things I could not give back. Nor
use. Or night or day or night or

loneliness. Other ways   feelings I could not
put into words   into themselves into people.
Blank monkeys of the hierachy. More deaths —
stupidity & death turning them on

into the beat of my droopy heart   my middle
passage blues my corroding hate my release
while I come to become neon iron eyes stainless lungs
blood zincgripped steel I
come up abstract

not able to take their bricks. Tar. Nor their flesh.
I ran: stung. Loop fumes hung
                              in my smoky lungs.

ideas I could not break nor form. Gave me
things I
see break & run down the crawling down the
game.

Illusion illusion, and you
would swear before screaming somehow
choked voices in me.

The crawling thing in the blood, the
huge immune loneliness. One becomes immune
to the bricks the feelings. One becomes
death.
One becomes each one and every person I
become. I could not
I COULD NOT
I could not whistle and walk in storms
along Lake Michigan's shore. Concrete walks.
I could not swallow the lake

ISOLATE

She knew more about me *than* let us say.
Most difficult, the American, she said.
Said a requiem is quite heavy, very dull and
These violet people in gentle expenditures!
                impossible to translate one:
Mass, and the day of masses.
Yet how was it to be ease for her, feeling
nothing of my spirit, knowing less of her own.

She knew only the visits to the tombs in me.
This pilgrimage she bled into her principles.
Higher, deeper than my closed eye.
Sees difficulty more in her "church" blood
                than in her cycle. & she started

on the birthcontrol pills again.
Some terrible romance of the flesh wedges us.
Here she was everything to me, after the crude
Cramming of Nothing; but now
I want isolation. I told her what.
She said, then isolate motherfucker

LONGLEGS

her Cool was a
northern thing
brought from the south

        she really stretched out in NYC

               long-
legs now step
silently in narrow streets
in the village

sleep on ease floors
dark travels on
high tongue eye trips
or the indispensable

devotion to music she
works for   her Cool

        she really stretches out like reels

in protective winter
nights her yoga and

diluted footfalls thru
parks of drums, night

challenge the tender pot
reek LSD, even beyond

to unknown codes on the
flesh of her reference

figures that rigid
situations put pressure

on   after all europe
mexico west coast & again NYC

could show her, define or should
necessarily   but she is

just a rapid position girl
change   case   move ment

of self efficient calm
in her private rites

SOMETHING IS EATING ME UP INSIDE

I go in & out a thousand times a day
& the round fat women with black velvet skin
expressions sit out on the
front steps, watching — "where does he go
so much" as if the knowledge could give meaning to
a hood from the 20s I look like in
my pocket black shirt button-down collar & black ivy
league. In & out to break the
agony in the pit of skull of fire for a drink a
cigarette bumming it anything the floor is
too depressing. I turn around inside the closet to search
the floor for a dime/ a nickel

this is from time & drunks of time again nights when
the pants pockets turned
inside turned
out but seriously something is
eating me up inside I don't
believe in anything anymore, science, magic —
in tape worms inside philosophy inside
I go outside

maybe inside you but not anybody else but
in the middle of going like
it's an inscrutable (what

ever
that
is)

something getting itself in deeper in. In,
time I mean pushing in against
my ear drums my time

— this is what I move full of,
slow young strong & sure of nothing myself a gangster
of the sunshine the sun is blood in my guts:
moving me from gin highs to lakesides to sit down
beside reasons for being in
the first place
in the second place looking
outward to definitions for definitions like

a formal ending would be unlawful unfair

KITCHEN CHAIR POEM #4

So they fought. not easy himself to
cope with. it was also around this time
that he began to really see. to ease up.
with a girl, this girl had been made &
the baby died: frail girl, alone in her small
room, if I remember. how strange, a small baby
who looked into something
motherlike. dumb. how strange the sticky candy
fingers, twisted. and the sour milk
all over her face.
She almost managed to live, growing into sticks,
small. some one once walked her in
a neglected park. like that, her teeth were soft
on nipples, they crumbled.
Somebody once walked her
in the neglected park: like that, and she buckled.
          Rolled over onto a radiator.
tiny ribs arms face grilling, frying
all night. the mother, drunk. wet with the fighter
still crawling in *his* sleep on her.
and the TV going. the roaches coming. so to speak
of hungry hustling broads.
still.
she had something going.
only you wouldn't come to it.

KITCHEN CHAIR POEM #5

a truck driver. 2nd floor roomer.
good for next months rent   ?
        a screaming silence fell down 3 flights and hit
the basement.   Couldn't last any longer.
her getting by, like. The jealousy. These others
with husbands who still had teeth.

every broad in the building screamed down
into her room. screaming on her
to make it, to get her hat.
scrape the wind outside. the blowing December slabs
nailed her against her
own desperation. and they had no idea

why she split without a fight. all those strikes
against her. like this dude said who just came
out of prison, giggling. Man I can't even afford
to look, with my eyes, funny.
but how could i tell him
her love had hit me the hardest? with my wife
standing inside my skull.

SEGREGATED SELF

he never knew she
hurt so way down the mother

level of self throb broke
between her and her

man who broke. she said
this memory of her happy self

a child, spaced.
(despite her mother

kicked gigantic holes in:
to her delicate

flesh, instinct. how-
ever she held now her man to-

gether what little was there
for the children. before

she stopped idealism said fuck
the hurt down at the mother

level the pain
he never knew that much

broke ran deep in her to try to
make ends meet to end

the failure of her-
self on the floor clutching

stink herself in the mirror
flies in the baby's mouth on the bottle

no he was so washed up he
left that kind of life.

grim as
what she is left with

THE GENERAL SENSE OF SELF

We weird thin   strangers
come
cloaked sighing in flesh
passionate sparetime lovers

with an irreversible perspective
and a pose
so solid
falling rain cannot charm its ghost

soaked in repressed rhythms
our life myths
are sunk in the useless riddle of
the emptiest excuses

these wornout and yet desperate artifacts
not enhancing our humanity   yet remain
imperishable as the idea of
killing food   killing for dreams

an irreversible point
of
view
so crisis-ridden that
the mystic work of our submission
to the huge color of ignorance
is never never   blasted
out of its monument
of soggy
and painful doubt

A POEM FOR AMERICANS AT THE TOP OF THE TV SCREEN
WHILE LOOKING DOWN INTO HELL

the clash
OF THE SKULL
imbedded:
(BIG FABRICMEDIA SYSTEMMIND
mythlanguage, caves recesses of
SHAPES: of ideas, the way ideas
doctor the sod of flesh,
intercourse shrines GRAFT
all that is saidtobe "sacred"
clash/ing into scripture of bones
forming fabric of
thot, the TVeye, a prophet
SHAPE inspired revelation
in the "system's own myth/language

him big ancient deity eating
ALL ALL, all of
it, cysts, too.

HERE

:the petrified forest of the
past, translates a clue to some
innermost jive adventure, or get to
such literal philosophy of the internal rhythm
of how the hazy dry fingers of muted ole
1890 Negroes could diagnose a banjo: or
talk about the mathematics of such captured minds
surviving easy, in rough prisons of the self just
outside incense kitchens sweeping out sweetpotato
and mustardgreen spells and odors: or briefly cop
the vernacular of some obscure, but eternal light
leaking thru the autumn dawn of some real forest
not yet created or invested with a purpose

FIT IN —

and sight the wonder of how
the edge of such an extension, bright blue
or dusty, without pregnancy: shows itself
clearly, shadow profile distance of the time it
takes this bright forward: facingclose, very close
up way people, like the eccentric black cat deep
in publicsocialmoral disgrace, he walks
talking insanely peculiar Everybody turn
around a living soul creature of a republic who
I keep trying to say to you is a wonder, too not
unlike sunblast fiesta extremes of rainbows, dropping
silence or flesh pushing away from noise organizing
it into control versions of any
coherence, a thing like twins who do not fit
into the same mantle, instruments or sacrifice

HER TONGUE QUICK

Her tongue, quick vivid!
quick
vivid
  snaps the smoke, ashes quick
vivid, told me, greeneyes watching
lyrics flesh lyrics of my
mouth, as it sees
  the snap twist of her tongue
quick/ vivid: how humor
ous. How serious. The effort

But "there are some passages
in your life, strange deadends which
can be understood, confirmed BUT
the rest of it, I just can't see how COME
in hell you weren't

burned a natural American death long ago.
you black prince you"

THE EGO AND SEX

the ego the ego play
for 2 surface persons   play the surface
of descriptive flesh, any flesh, my
   eyes institutions of
primary holes   of the ego playing holes
in merry flesh   primarily of love on
                    on the dark structure of
   the implicit geography that is
                 between the described
     flesh; the holes,
hips, arms   the numerous holes, hips, arms
  of=   MARY WARMTH   =of
2 egos, movements, properly in motion pri-
mary animation of purely proper
             darkest, swiftest
         unending flesh of human intellectual
hunger, in merriest flesh, the
   darkness of a primary timeless rehearsal to
sustain, to unsurface infanticide, to
   primarily exist, to be of the essence of warmth as
             these fleshy castles of 2
   below the surface and
correspondingly climaxing "people" trip, as
   the play attacks itself and primarily begins this
        way

SWAN GENTLENESS : the gentry lie

the unspoken pledge to super-
ficial shoddy "gods here
is a terrible usury
in/which the witches, these vultures
feel apprehension but not enough
disenchantment.

Rich queens suck the blood of dishwashers;
the guilt, frustration, they leave to their
        lackies. They do not speak the pledge
,it is ungodly to speak these witches
never get to the point. Distracted radicals
stumble in white cities blinded by the ancient walls.

                                (and these
rich bitches stumble free though in shadows deep
whores losing synonyms of self never mothers nor
perfect whores even just studded with the weight
of their crowns, just artifacts. The format
of dead reference. They do not fall

down and break their crowns. The pledge distracts,
they are vultures of virtue.

A POEM AMERICANS ARE GOING TO HAVE TO MEMORIZE SOON

              these huge teachable slangy people
touched with giddy shallowness (dig

    the substance of American Humor, defraud
    even plants in their own humble sunlight
    like in apartment windows, even parcels
    for real people who go deep,
    in irregular bareness even into some gods or the mind
become
                  monstrosities, you know
money, chairs and things like the meaning of other
people are not even accessable DESTRUCTION here)

             threadbare in this revolution
now submissively jump into some cold practice,

    brash enough to have appointments
    official like, while I lay up digging this shit

OUTLINE OF SOME PRIVATE SOUNDS
— to memory of Alma

you ain't worth shit, baby
OUTLINE coming on with shape & jive so thick
:that greasy advantage you
use, practice. You scribble
on some white folks post card, WISH YOU WERE HERE
& note the menu, say in your gainful
letters WHEN THEY GONNA GET REALLY
DOWN WITH SOME waste SOUL EATS
I)tho lockedup in profound abstraction, some-
time such complete locks doors deep grease
of you, the shape of such outlines
so private, my skill to see, exist turns) but
despite sham (I get to you
YOU CHISEL, wax eyes going HUH?
WHAT DID YOU SAY & you know, shit you the expert!
at cheap schemes, the only real enterprise you
got is your genetic crevice, which you
can't even instruct.

VIEWPOINTS

stimulate a viewpoint in viewpoint minds,
& such canny concerns are fumbled points
media press souls for time & draw the outlines
in love & money, around the impotence of ideas
of each man person installment on flesh or animal
going into the fundamental weight light strain
of space known as cities behind apartments behind
radios TVs newsprint bled white from bowels of
trees waves like sex forming grief the ideas of soul
or half the ebb of any formation even how chopped
chives in cream cheese should speak out of the
context of politics drain at any price the net
of human gentle weight how the mind should or
should not pitch the ball with acute love death as it
describes failure or a dreamy land of ghosts in
a rain deep blue land or what nouns should be
stuffed into so much unendurable pyscho-
sleep sonata) therapy is one way to point
at the afterall immaterial view, vitals.

SELF WORLD

can redwhite & blue I enter
some self, the self
of some-
body
;myself   ?   in pure flesh & mind love
all of me   ?
Sounds silly
but read again, & enter yourself, to
see as I see

MY 3 YEAR OLD BLACK EYES
TRAGIC, BEAUTIFUL PAIN
LOOKING FROM THOSE YEARS
such a photo

define this trembling nation, the
sacred "untouchable
insanity. (Concessions

A coldturkey promise, myself. Some face, image
can this image, red white & blue
enter
these monsters, they use deodorant,
and brush their teeth.
And do not know
anything, even as I explain

                                        myself. Or
language, how it is our beauty
            true in
            MY 3 YEAR OLD BLACK EYES
            TRAGIC, BEAUTIFUL PAIN
            LOOKING FROM THOSE YEARS
same as   now

ABBREVIATION OF THE BLUES

he like modesty comes out of a cloister
what, 22 or
just out of college limbo with white irregularity
from the wretched asylum of a ghetto
young mississippi, the voice so soft

you could break it with your efficiency anytime
he like slate, noiseless (not even San Francisco quite
put city blood loud impotence in
his repressed encampment of anger, but
you could see him dignified come on beautifully

in the shameless standup moments of crushing mississippi
calmly down with love, but never to back
down into its blond hardness, even while
abstract accumulations of so much confusion of
clairvoyant insight, & neglected intellectual excitement

left him writing like a clerk secret prefaces to
his disguised bitterness, found him pumping
in street demonstrations to make sure of his belief in
some semblance of anything pushed far away
from the rusty possibility of some ancient African egoism

AIR

breathing   the breath.   clearance   .the air
the air, the breathing air.   The math of the
    air the figures of breathing the mind
        the science of things, the
men, the life, ring repeat in/out breathing life
men give to air, the breath   .Clearance, a
clear
convincing math of things. OUT IN THE COUNTRY.
Trees, some irregular plants. Not here, now:
THIS CITY. of destruction to breathing, to hands
even, eyelids that cover the sounds, to lips that
pave the pavement of flesh to the air, to the
way we walk, OUT IN THE COUNTRY to get air. The
kind of hands that touch, break sink into soft
mud, out
there

under eyelids.

PART TWO

WAITING IN THE CHILDREN'S HOSPITAL
(1957)

I reflect on this desperate note
while waiting in the children's hospital.
The desperate cry my son left
cold as ice in his closed eyes after poison.

Benches of blood. This is a wooden tragedy.

Joyce & I walked home under the huge night
thru a grand rain sweep and
around midnight I scribble a letter to my sister,
who is dying five minutes at a time:
      You are the flower of confusion
      coming up in the morning
      of my love and
      going tightly shut in the afternoon of
      anger. Anger & bitterness.
                I look forward to your resurrection.

I get up tonight and walk naked
through the wet weeds. The moon is smiling
and it has no teeth.

I walk home less, the huge night in me.

I remember a trillion stars in the Lexington night
above all shadows ahead of me but
I cannot remember the feeling
of a little girl's kiss.   Do you remember?

I remember I walked to town with a blind
man beside me singing or was he humming.

41

That same summer of a trillion grasshoppers. And
I loved him through & beyond his blackness.
His woman in a shack beside the highway
with four grandbabies in a wooden bed;
fanning summer flies from the syrup on their lips.

But the blood is white this summer.

Roasted ears. The hog season & my uncle
was a good shot. The blood is red this summer
redder than redbirds.

I felt that I had to go along in silence
with the heart of a monk, face flat to the earth
arms outstretched. & when I got up
I walked close to walls.
I moved with my head low and my hands hidden
like a starved Christian, meaning
to do this forever.

THE REVERED BLACK WOMAN
— for Abby Lincoln

O sad true image-maker
deep shades of blue, deep shades of blue
I say to you: (in your ache
        afro-blue, afro you
        mater . . .
        afro-blue, afro you
        — an instrumental universal institutional
        soul poet, don't Let Up.
        Teach me my emotional shallowness.
        Teach me my message, only you know.
        From your black breasts. Melodies of hurt.
        Tender ache, afro-blue, afro you.
I hear music — I hear trumpets, guitars
— pianos, bass, and I hear magic demonstrations
        in the muse — in the human voice, the black
        — sweet jazz singers' afro blue tone.
        The she-determined sinuous
          interpretation. Softly,
O sad, sad magic maker, blue mother.

VIETNAM

he was just back
from the war

said man they got
whites

over there now
fighting
us

and blacks over there
too

fighting us

and we can't tell
our whites
from the others

nor our blacks
from the others

& everybody
is just killing

& killing
like crazy

CONTINUED RICH PLUNGES

In the muted prices of
Vacation
Escape from   the shattering experience of
Autumn's Big Moment
The subtle truth is that there is
No relaxation in the mystery
Of the valley of the future
Every day is magic

RAKISH ANGLE

Come dance my caution — wife
regular lips, rose tinted rememberance of
paid-ways. Come fly my smooth cabs of fun;
gaze at breaking edges until eyes
know water of shapes steely sheen. Come
explore — passengers on their way to actual . . .
taunt beginnings   failures.
Then come and join group marriage.
Plan to join us soon.

CREED

You were so unsure of me
you asked questions I sought
you thru the human without illustrations
you were so reluctant I said to hell
with dissenters you I feel rivers of you coming
to me to rivet my core into your targets of silver

but knowing your battled home destroyed some
                     of your goods while it ENGRAVED UPON
                     THE TIME THE FORMAT OF YOUR DISTINCT
                     QUALITY
they are freaks
I tried to tell you
they are freaks baby
don't let them get next to you they are freaks so

motionless lost long players stale age
                 keep your sight
                 there is a white winter? SNOW
                 & in it you sd: "is romance like
                 being a host or something

extraordinary (like me   behind black glasses &
because I was not lighthearted you have begun
to die of happiness

INTERIOR
— for Sheila

You and I move
our eyes   our level
thru wet snow
calmly between   inhuman buildings
they have not yet
decided to make art
                (in fluffy coats we clutch
my direction   figuring
out one rapid
transit into
the uptown dreary landscape blind against central
park)   traveling
impossible walks with
only the formless warmth of each
restaurant or memory of
                ourselves together later eating
liver and the
smallest tomatoes I have ever seen while Bob
Dylan cries and groans on the radio you
do your
paper game against the ruined head
                of American history
we lie down eye level in
the peppermint cloth we see
up yet know form
less kindness of our
                together distance beauty or we
rap
rapidly out of amazement at the high
function of our sweet
innocent minds lower

into the heart we
cop together the interior of our
energy of our
reference our love
neat essence embraces without struggle our
symbolism or to put it simply you
saw in some
future dropping
back into the mixture of these
        delicate moments the
soft durable weight of our
        lives, anytime.

EGYPTIANS

She has raped
            Him.
He is no longer
              of
a big order
in his inertness
his eyes close
                & die.
His seed
went thru a flower,
into the womb &
brought forth
              Power:
Spirit & Intelligence

His kind
           did not die.
But she lived
to see
        All.

LINE

there is a line on
the sky. It is not
the kind of line I

said. But blacksmoke
from a metal object
moving, there is no
scar on any bitch.
Strange that I take
all the words back,
now. But not the
rose, nor the bush.

I remember the bush,
and whores now are
real, not dreams.

THE AGONY OF PAIN

around the hospital an interpreter of pain
wanders in a mosquito net.
His eyes are two fat Women. His civilization
is in his pocket and his precious
English Language is Dead now that America "is free."
But he uses it anyway. His friends are dead.
The enthusiastic war killed them.
Around Africa — his body is shaped like the map of Africa —
he wears a large admiration belt to hold up the net.
The administration of the hospital is sound and
from all appearances the interpreter of pain
will have a job nightmare after nightmare,
as long as howling men cannot explain their depth.
Death is nothing.

THE DOLL BELIEVERS

This lifeless construction,
Yellow hair curled and twisted,
The forever motionless face of rubber,
The dark marked eyebrows,
The pug nose of flexible material,
Spongy cheeks painted red,
Camel-hair eyebrows moving up and down.
Lifting her up, the eyes fly open,
They stare into space unmoved,
Those deep blue and soft eyes,
Those never winking, moving balls,
Controlled from the inside,
And that thick rubber body,
The imprint of a navel,
The undersized hands,
The thick soft knees,
The screwed-on head,
The air hole behind her neck,
All this in its lifelessness
Gives me a feeling that children
Are really powerful people
To imagine that such a thing
Could be alive.

DANGER ZONE

If I were adequately armed
And the kind of decision that makes
Or breaks the settlement of
    human arms and human galilees
Would finally mean rejection of Myself
Anyway; would it not? Would it not?
Force is no column of answers for Fear.
There exist little streams of invasions
    for impending Numbers to fill the gap
And supply the risk we take with Ventures
Fully in command of their own endings: armed
& ready to die for what Nobody Now believes in.

MEETING

some members of a reported
& united plight
& myself:
it just wasn't the sort of thing you would expect
from a turnedon &
borrowed crisp woman, a "lady"
who came down
from the bottom of her rich money
& suddenly talked the
beginning of politics into
what I was thinking
all along

which was not her ass

she sat still
locked away
  in her own mystery where
no eye looked from
  her meaning in
us while pain danced an
      ugly step
around her frail
    CONCLUSIONS

      there are
      those who swipe her
        human definition push
      her away from the
:center

of herself those who
      in their inhuman hunger
      nibble at the
beautiful crust of her invisible initials
like
a sea of fire upon the body of
a martyr
as she struggles
   to the   CENTER   of herself
the bloodymurder
of those form[   ]less "obstacles"
of the deepest silence
   in the heart of consciousness
play
heavy devil games in
her sleep in her

56

deep richCLEAR face in
the mother
palms of her
        hands anywhere

                getting to her
                even in the frustrated riddle
of technology
:that (   ) theoretically
        protects her in
her
                !inscrutable "history"

IT WAS

some sense that a whole
generation, & not
for the first time

knows defeat." I
knew even then that it
was whole world

taking place in just
my mind. Sense of
some invalid bullshit.

it was a long
time before I saw
anything. Like

a seashore, even
the stockyards 5
blocks away. But

close, and not
a lie: was the
pool of blood —

animal blood. I saw
a long line of gulls
early, taste now
even their cry.

But none of it is
fumbled together,
reflecting some-

thing singular. Nor
was there in any
of it, a crisis.

I WAS

I said I was the night
to try to be it. Magic
a collision of black

music, midnight allies
when I said I screwed
a girl, late at night.

While a Baptist Church
talked thru its loud
speaker. I said it all.

MY SEASONAL BODY, MY EARS

6 months I was in
the ratio of the weight of myself,
in myself calm sad by volume

substance and volume. Some kind
of soldier who could not clean the
lonely hospital hall from

the spirit of my one hundred
& fifty pounds, with light finding
the regular shapes out of the strange

natural chestful of sour oranges I
remember each elastic moment
of each grave space of my solitary cold

stay. Warm locality the sky, boats or sea
out so heavy, lonesome far to land stood
then the perfect rotunda of all the time

left in me, 16 years old: the holes fragments
in my head, eyes so desolate, the weight
of myself so young so yearning

UNEXPECTED LOVE

unexpected assistance
like a female sponsor at the baptism of my life,
shines like lustrous —
precious yellow metallic elements, not yet even conceived!
A good Supreme Deity, perhaps.
No? Now who is this. Hands, heart & heavy love —
so tender rendered unexpected assistance *as* love.
It does actually physically shine, like I feel luck
shines like metallic elements, lustrous —
yet
I am a new black man, new and deeper in darkness.
I am still intramural. And the walls of this ghost city
are still closed on a precious forest of vision

ON THE FIRST WAKE UP OF LIGHT, IT'S DEATH.

                             the presence of color seems
to outbreak, light
                      never beginning,
erupting no end into
                      bleak Chicago South Side
    wipe out elicit dump black strength of
storedup streets   impressions outcome.

Sundaymorn   all that careful waste-
d   human effusion, from those Saturdaynight
        parties: the presence of

this rubbermetalglass mathematical mobile, Ford
      outshining/ growing into distance/timing
          oozing, discharging, trickling
          BANG! !
                  (unconscious
          CRASH! !
death)

    There was a chubby black woman. She is
now this chubby black woman, with party partypaper
                  cap on her booze, herbs-stained
cells, the x quality that everybody everywhere I
think
    have been so concerned about. Is now
looking into to see, the presence of
        but can't